HOW TO BUILD A
CAR

Quarto is the authority on a wide range of topics.
Quarto educates, entertains and enriches the lives of our readers—
enthusiasts and lovers of hands-on living.
www.quartoknows.com

6 Orchard Road, Suite 100
Lake Forest, CA 92630
quartoknows.com
Visit our blogs @quartoknows.com

MIX
Paper from
responsible sources
FSC® C017606

Printed in China
3 5 7 9 10 8 6 4 2

HOW TO BUILD A
CAR

Written by SASKIA LACEY

Illustrated by MARTIN SODOMKA

TABLE OF CONTENTS

Meet The Scrap Pack!. 6

Step 1: Dream 9

Step 2: Build the Frame. 16

Step 3: Build the Engine. 24

Step 4: Build the Body 42

Step 5: Hit the Road! 54

Nuts and Bolts. 56

How to Build a Car in 5 Steps 62

Eli's New Dream. 64

MEET THE SCRAP PACK!

Eli

The Dreamer

The king of crazy ideas, creativity is Eli's specialty.

Most likely to: Make a mess

Favorite car: Corvette ZR1

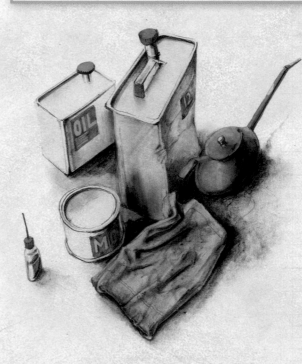

Phoebe
The Mechanic
The smarty-pants with nitty-gritty know-how about cars.
Most likely to: Build something that actually works
Favorite car: Rolls Royce Wraith

Hank
The Jewel of the Junkyard
The frog with "junk connections" and access to high-quality scraps.
Most likely to: Go dumpster diving
Favorite car: Jaguar C-X75

Step 1: Dream

Eli had a new idea. A huge, **speedy** idea. An idea that would take him places. It was his best idea yet. Or at least he hoped so.

But this wasn't the sort of project a mouse could take on alone. Eli would need an extra set of paws. Maybe even two.

He knew just who to ask. His best friends, Hank and Phoebe.

But there was one problem. Hank and Phoebe didn't like Eli's ideas. Probably because they usually led to trouble. The mouse would need to choose just the right moment to ask for their help.

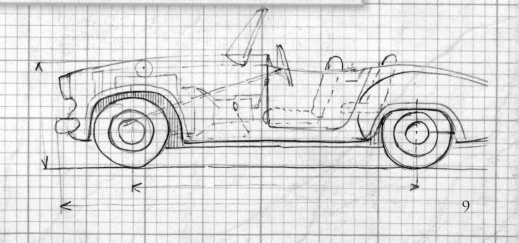

The moment came when they were arguing about cars.

"Nothing's cooler than a Jaguar!" Hank croaked. "Admit it!"

"I'll never admit it," Phoebe said. "Because it isn't true. The Rolls Royce? Now that's traveling in style!"

The two friends turned to Eli, but he was too busy thinking to take sides. "We should build our own car!" he announced. Hank and Phoebe blinked at him in silence.

"That's the craziest idea I've ever heard!" Phoebe exclaimed.

"Don't you want to see the world?" Eli asked. "Let's hit the road and feel the wind in our fur."

"I don't have fur!" Phoebe protested.

"This is a great idea!" Eli pleaded.

"Do you remember your last great idea?" Phoebe asked gently.

"Yes," Eli said, looking down at his feet. "Hank almost exploded."

"Yes! I almost exploded." Hank cried. "Exploded!"

"Rocket-powered roller skates seemed like a good idea at the time," Eli muttered.

"What about the ice cream slingshot you made before that?" Phoebe continued. "My feathers were sticky for two whole weeks."

"OK, OK. I get it," Eli said glumly. "You guys are right. It's a crazy idea."

12

Eli told himself that he would absolutely, positively not think about building a car. Instead he would only think practical, non-car-related thoughts.

But it was useless. Eli had cars on the brain. **Wheels! Bumpers! Horns!** High-speed chases filled his mind. He had to build a car.

Eli decided to work on changing Hank's mind first. If he could just get him excited, the frog might have a change of heart.

"Hank, how's business?" Eli asked.

"Just another day at the junkyard. You know how it is." Hank sounded glum.

"It can get boring doing the same thing, day after day," said Eli. "It would be great if we could get out of town and take a break from this dump."

"You're telling me," said Hank.

"Hey, Hank," Eli took a deep breath. It was now or never. "I still really want to build a car. You know, if we had a car, we could get out and explore the world."

"I don't know." Hank scratched his head. "Your ideas never work out very well—especially for me."

"Please, Hank!" the mouse begged. "I promise things will be different this time. PLEASE?"

"Maybe." Hank shook his head. "But you've got to promise NO rockets!"

"Deal!" the mouse said excitedly.

"I can't believe I'm doing this again," Hank groaned.

Step 2: Build the Frame

The two friends got right to work. Hank found an old frame at the junkyard. Eli called Phoebe in to see it. Maybe if she saw how serious they were, she would help them build the car.

"This is a fine frame. I'm impressed," said Phoebe. "Are you still planning to build the car?"

Eli could tell that Phoebe was trying hard not to sound curious. "Hank thinks it's worth a try," he said. "But we really need someone who knows cars inside and out. I don't know if we'll get very far by ourselves. Do you think you could possibly, just this once, help with a crazy idea?"

"I'll think about it," said Phoebe.

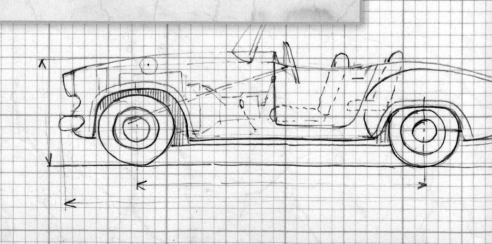

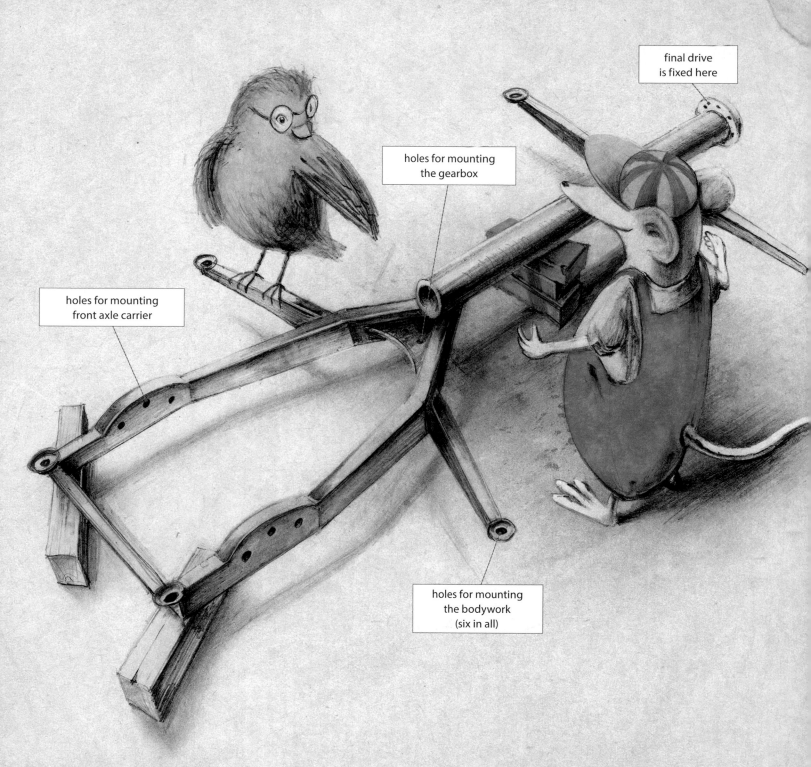

17

FRONT SUSPENSION

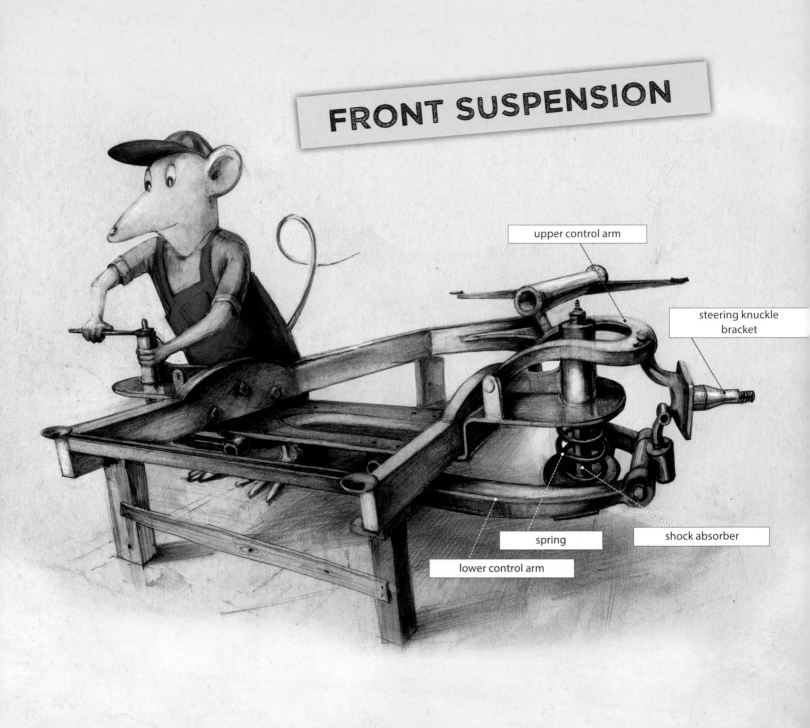

upper control arm

steering knuckle bracket

spring

lower control arm

shock absorber

When Phoebe showed up the next day, Eli and Hank grinned. She had already started mapping out the chassis.

"Phoebe, you came!" Hank whooped. "The Scrap Pack is all here!"

"Don't get too excited," warned Phoebe. "I'm only staying if we do this the right way. Not the crazy Eli way."

"I promise," Eli grinned. "You're in charge!"

All About the Frame

The frame is the foundation of the car. It provides support and strength for the rest of the vehicle, just like a skeleton holds up the mechanic's body.

Before the three friends knew it, they were almost finished building the chassis.

"It's already starting to look like a real car!" Eli squeaked happily.

"Where should we go first?" Hank asked excitedly. "The beach?"

"I've never seen the ocean!" said Eli. "Let's go!"

"Hold up," Phoebe interrupted. "We're not going anywhere until we build the engine."

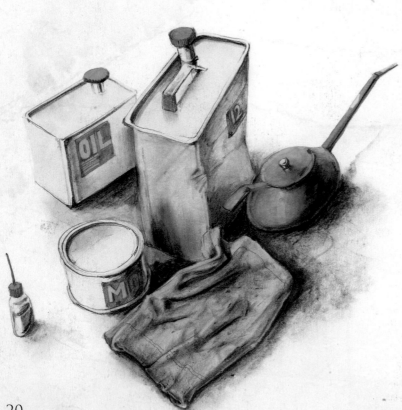

CHASSIS

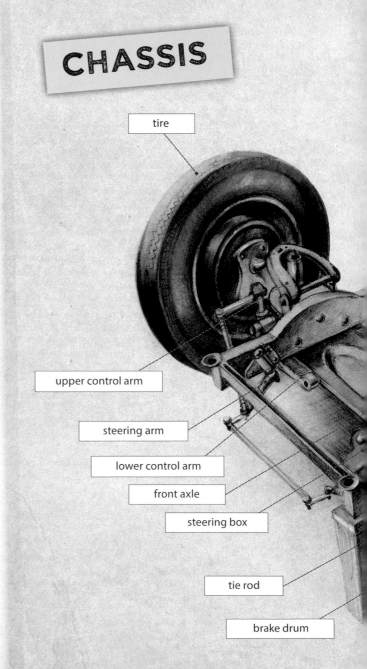

tire

upper control arm

steering arm

lower control arm

front axle

steering box

tie rod

brake drum

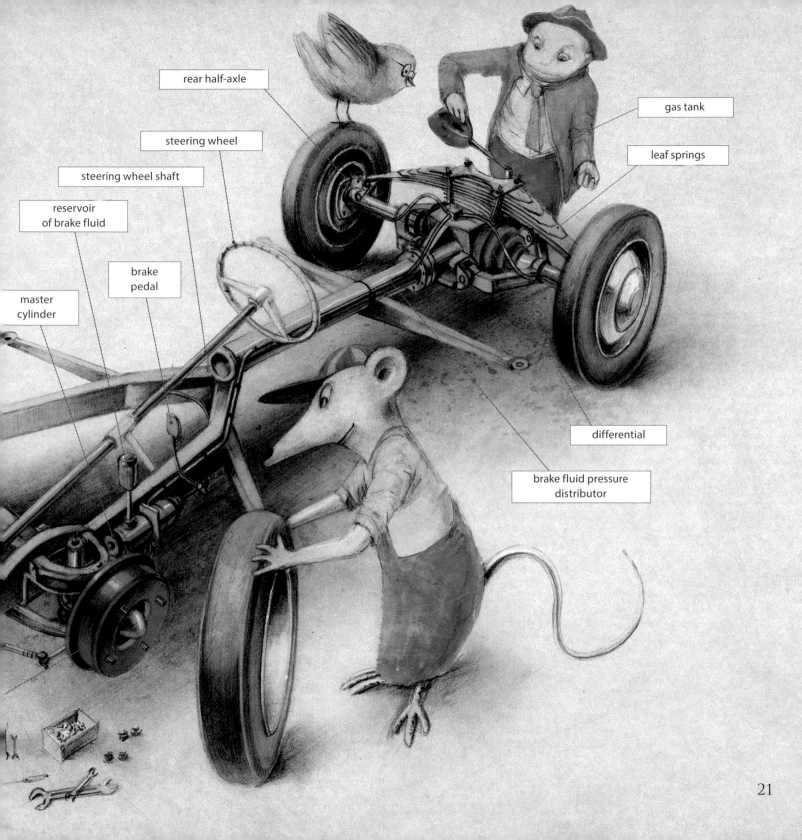

rear half-axle

steering wheel

steering wheel shaft

reservoir
of brake fluid

brake
pedal

master
cylinder

gas tank

leaf springs

differential

brake fluid pressure
distributor

21

"OK," said Eli. "But before we start on the engine, I thought maybe we could talk about some new ideas I have for the car."

"Are these good ideas or Eli ideas?" Phoebe laughed.

"Um…" Eli paused. He wasn't sure. "Maybe both?"

"Just let him tell us!" said Hank.

"I was thinking we could build **ejector seats** into the car. That way we could make a quick escape—"

"NO, Eli!" shrieked Hank. "No ejector seats!"

"What about **laser beams**?" Eli said hopefully.

"Oooh! I like laser beams!" said Phoebe.

Hank did not look pleased.

"Don't worry, I'll stay focused," said Eli. "Ejector seats are out! Got it."

Step 3: Build the Engine

Eli couldn't believe that they were already working on the engine. It was all coming together, just as he had dreamed!

Rev It Up

The engine is like the brain of the car. It controls how fast or slow the car moves. In order for an engine to run, it needs to burn fuel. The engine's carburetor uses electricity to ignite the fuel.

FOUR-STROKE ENGINE CYCLE

1	2	3	4
intake	compression	power	exhaust

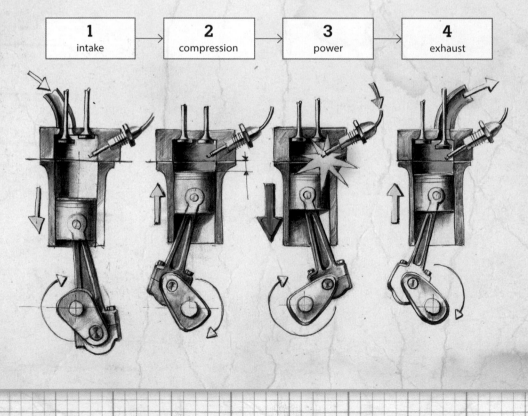

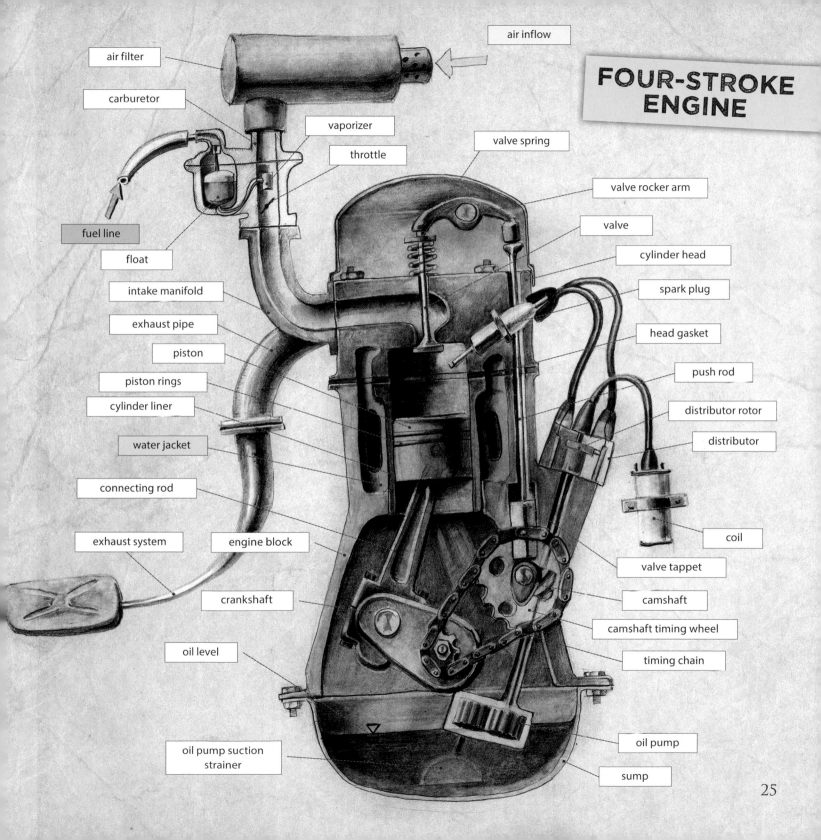

air filter

air inflow

carburetor

FOUR-STROKE ENGINE

vaporizer

throttle

valve spring

valve rocker arm

valve

fuel line

cylinder head

float

spark plug

intake manifold

head gasket

exhaust pipe

piston

push rod

piston rings

distributor rotor

cylinder liner

distributor

water jacket

connecting rod

coil

exhaust system

engine block

valve tappet

crankshaft

camshaft

camshaft timing wheel

oil level

timing chain

oil pump suction strainer

oil pump

sump

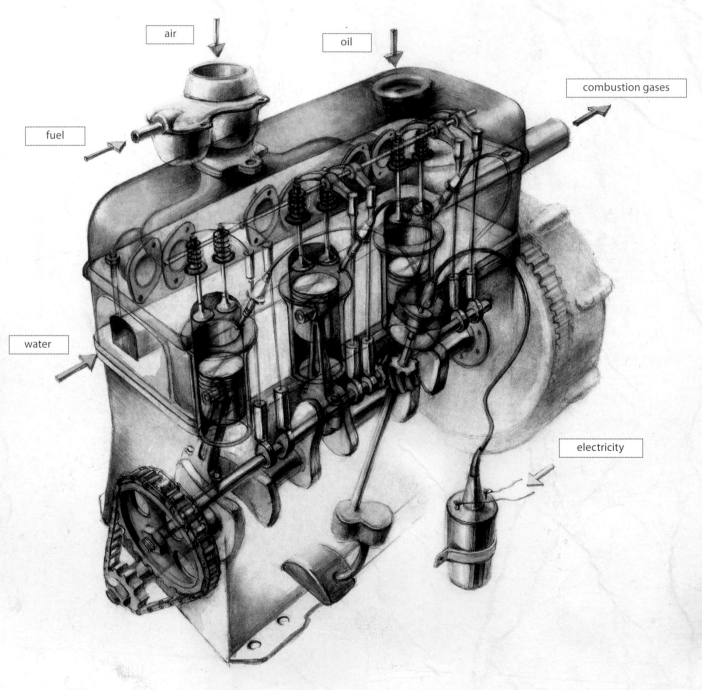

air

oil

combustion gases

fuel

water

electricity

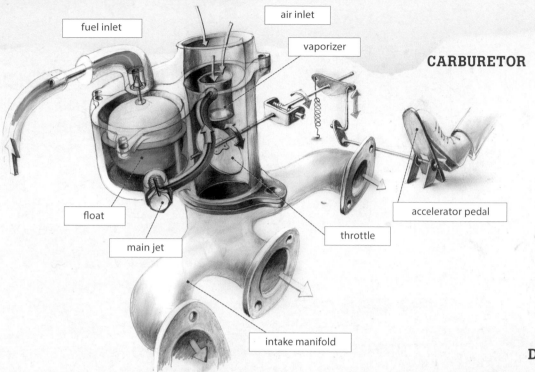

CARBURETOR

fuel inlet

air inlet

vaporizer

float

main jet

throttle

accelerator pedal

intake manifold

DISTRIBUTOR

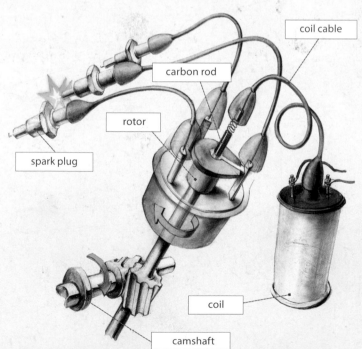

coil cable

carbon rod

rotor

spark plug

coil

camshaft

Building an engine was more complicated than he had ever imagined, but it was almost complete. Eli was doing his best to keep his crazy ideas to himself. It was hard, because he had a different idea every minute, and he wanted to share them all with his best friends. But he knew making a regular engine was complicated.

When all the parts were in place, Phoebe hooted, "It's engine time! Are you guys ready to drop it into the chassis?"

"Ready as ever," said Eli. "I just need to get some boxes to stand on. Hank is like 10 inches taller than me."

"I'm not that tall."

"Yes, you are!" Phoebe and Eli said at the same time.

Carefully...carefully...the engine was slowly lowered into the frame. The three animals cheered!

MOUNTING THE ENGINE AND GEARBOX

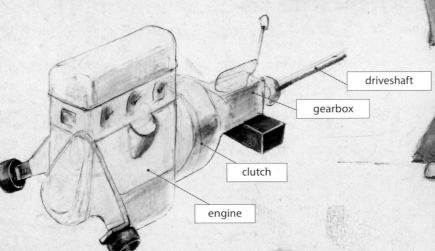

driveshaft

gearbox

clutch

engine

exhaust manifold

fan belt

cold water inlet from the radiator

**MOUNTING THE ENGINE
ONTO THE CHASSIS**

inlet
manifold

hot water outlet to radiator

cylinder head

water pump pulley

alternator pulley

fuel pump

crankshaft pulley

engine mount

29

They stepped back to admire their work. "Man, is it ever hot," said Hank. "Please tell me this car is going to have a cooling system. We don't want the engine to overheat!"

"I've already got it in the plans!" Phoebe smiled.

Eli watched as the radiator was attached to the car. This car wasn't going to get stuck on the side of the road!

Keepin' Your Cool

Powerful engines get really hot! A proper cooling system keeps the engine cool and running smoothly.

radiator

fan

air filter

universal joint

ENGINE WATER COOLING SYSTEM

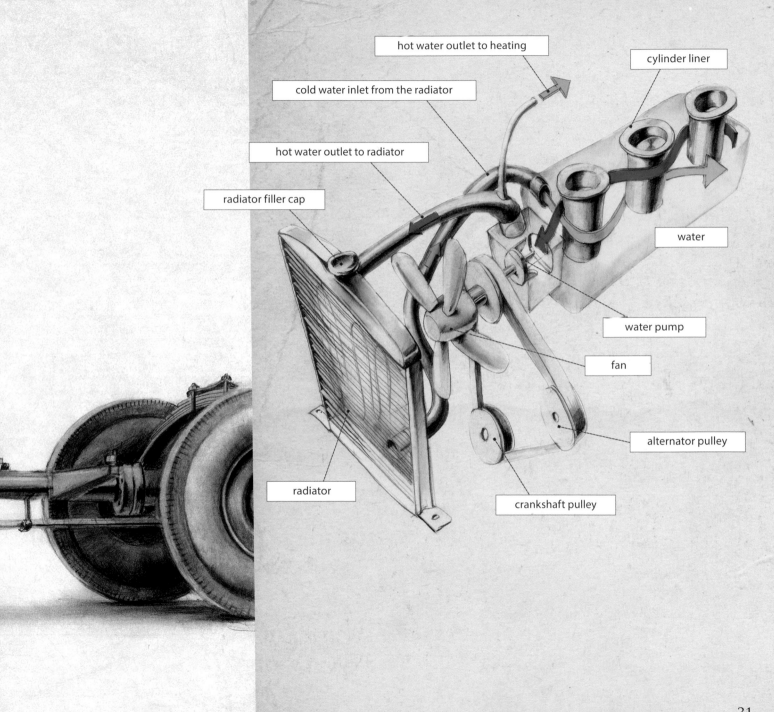

hot water outlet to heating

cold water inlet from the radiator

cylinder liner

hot water outlet to radiator

water

radiator filler cap

water pump

fan

alternator pulley

radiator

crankshaft pulley

That evening, after a long day of hard work, Eli relaxed by doing his favorite thing—thinking about cars. And for the first time in his life, he wasn't just thinking about the cars on the road, he was envisioning his very own dream car. There was still so much to build. They needed to work on the body, attach the wheels, and design the interior. Eli couldn't wait to get back to the garage!

dynamo

clutch pedal

brake pedal

But the next day, Eli found his two friends arguing about the car.

"I can't believe you lost the drawings I made of the body!" Phoebe griped.

"You try keeping track of everything in this junkyard," Hank replied.

"What's going on?" Eli asked.

"This isn't a scrap pack. It's just a mess!" Phoebe chirped a *harrumph* and flew away.

Hank wandered into the garage. "Sorry, pal. I thought maybe this time one of your crazy plans might actually work."

The mouse watched sadly as Hank hopped away.

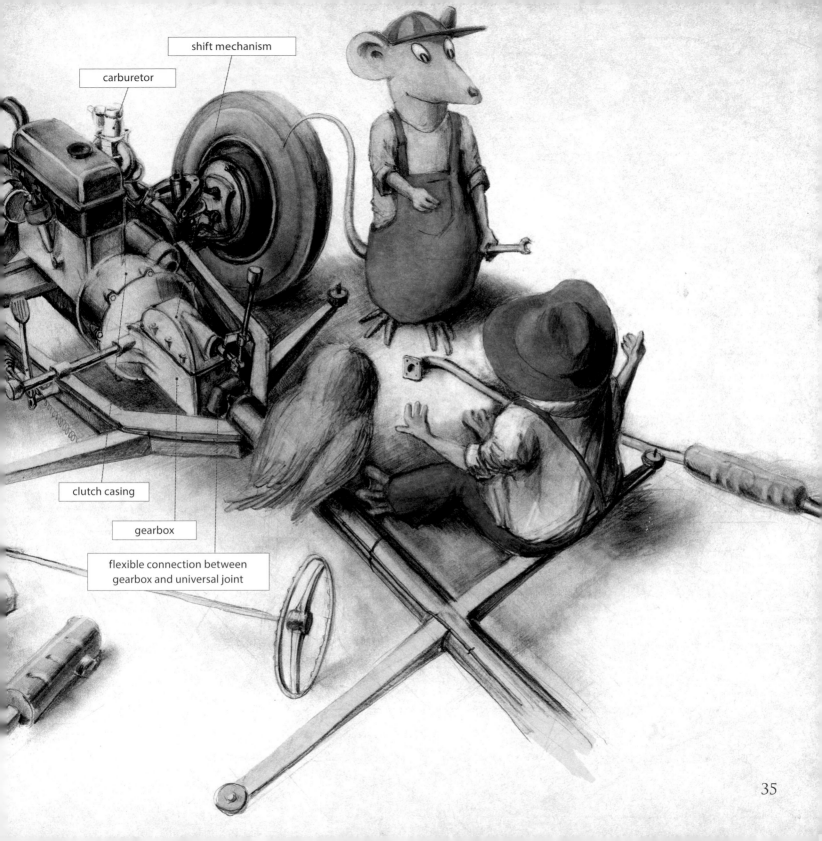

carburetor

shift mechanism

clutch casing

gearbox

flexible connection between gearbox and universal joint

35

Eli spent the whole night thinking. He needed to solve this problem. If he didn't, Hank and Phoebe might give up. It wouldn't matter that they had the engine done, if they couldn't figure out how to build the rest of the car.

"Stay focused," Eli muttered to himself. "Think of a **practical solution**."

Eli tried to pretend he was Phoebe, a practical, focused problem solver. But it was hard! Eli wasn't Phoebe. Soon the mouse found himself daydreaming about cars made of cheese and racetracks in the sky.

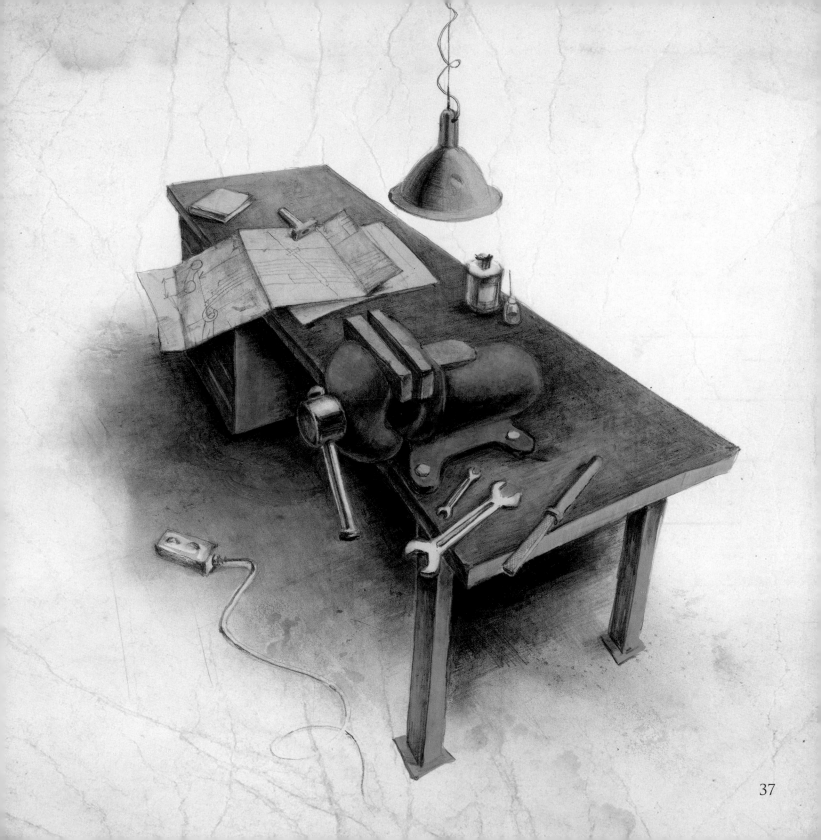

That was it! They couldn't drive in the sky. But maybe they could do the next best thing. What if they skipped the roof and built a convertible? Maybe, just maybe, it would work.

The next day, Eli called the team in to hear his plan. Hank and Phoebe listened.

They shared a look. Then Hank broke the silence. "Are you thinking what I'm thinking?"

"You've done it, Eli!" Phoebe cheered. "This will make the whole project easier."

Phoebe and Hank promised Eli they would build a convertible. Hank said, "You're finally going to feel the wind in your fur!"

"You guys are the best! And I've brought in some more friends to help us finish the job," said Eli. "The Scrap Pack just got bigger and better! I don't know about you, but I'm ready to hit the road."

"Let's do this!" they all cheered.

Step 4:
Build the Body

Eli and the rest of the team set to work on building the body of the car. This was the part Eli had been looking forward to the most. He knew the other parts of the car were important, but he was excited to finally be making his dream project look the way it should— **ZOOM-TASTIC**!

Ain't She a Beauty!

The body of the car is made up of the doors, windows, and large panels of metal that hold all the pieces together. It keeps everyone inside the car safe. And car maniacs can obsess over making it look beautiful!

Soon it was time to paint the body. The Scrap Pack had decided to paint the car sky blue.

"Careful not to get any paw prints in the paint!" Phoebe reminded the team.

But Eli barely heard her. He was too busy daydreaming about where their car would take them.

Next they mounted the body onto the chassis. It was really, REALLY heavy.
"One, two, three…lift!" Phoebe called out from above.
"Squeak, squeak, squeak," the mice grunted.
"Croak, croak, croak," Hank huffed.
With a loud thud, everything fell into place.

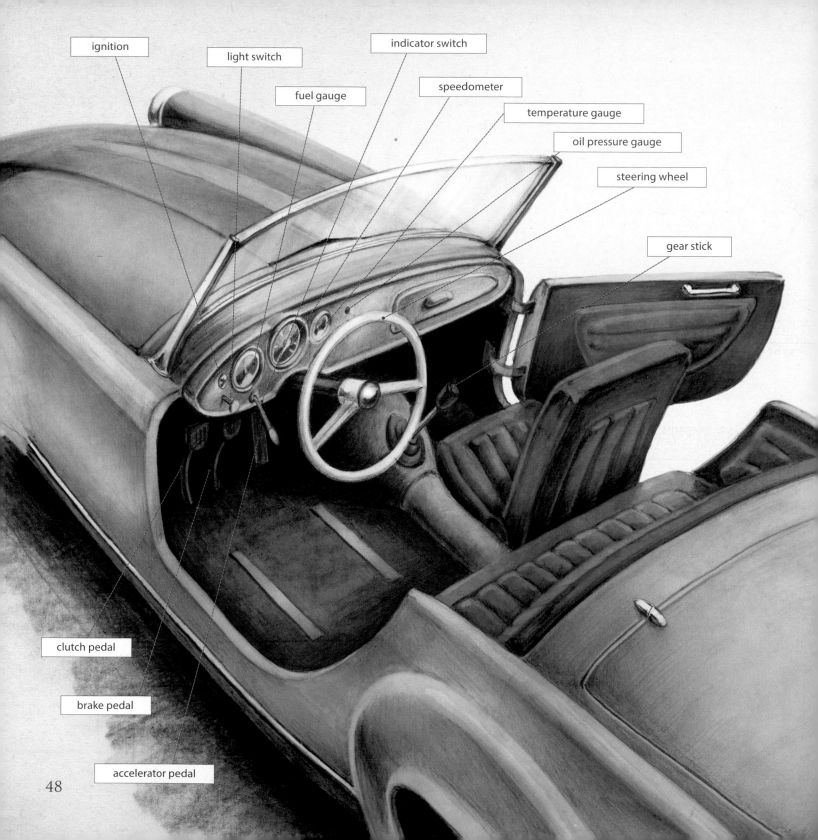

ignition

light switch

indicator switch

fuel gauge

speedometer

temperature gauge

oil pressure gauge

steering wheel

gear stick

clutch pedal

brake pedal

accelerator pedal

48

"All that's left now are the finishing touches," Phoebe said.

"I have the perfect seats in the back," said Hank. He dragged four plush seats over from his pile of parts.

The three friends loaded the seats, dashboard, and dozens of buttons and knobs into the car.

It's What's Inside that Counts

The engine powers the car, but primo leather seats and all the right bells and whistles make a car fun to drive. The speedometer, temperature gauge, and gas levels tell drivers everything they need to know to hit the road.

"I think it's time to name the car," said Eli. What about Bartholomew?"

"No way. That's awful," said Phoebe. "What about Theodora?"

"That's worse! Maybe we should ask Hank."

"Hank will just want to name the car after himself!"

"Hey, that's a good idea!" said Eli.

"What is?" Phoebe asked.

"We could name the car after ourselves. Like combine our names into one name."

"I like that idea!" Phoebe said.

"What about Phelank?" Eli proposed.

"That's a good one!"

"Or Helibee?" Eli said.

"Nice!"

Hank joined in on the fun. "I've got an idea for a name. Elephank! This car is huge—just like an elephant!"

"I love Elephank!" Eli jumped up and down. Three votes for Elephank?"

The other animals nodded. The car had been named, and Elephank was born.

It was finally time to test the engine. The pack held their breath. Eli's ears flew open when he heard Elephank's first **VROOM VROOM**. It was the sweet sound of success.

Step 5: Hit The Road!

The big day had finally come. The Scrap Pack was out on the open road, and it was even better than Eli had imagined. The wind was in his fur. His friends were by his side. Eli didn't know where they were going, but he had some great ideas!

Nuts and Bolts

Take a closer look at the parts and pieces that make up a car!

DRUM BRAKE

Need to slow down or stop when you're on the road? Then you'd better have a drum brake. When a driver pushes on the brake pedal, the brake shoes clamp against the spinning brake drum. This slows the car down.

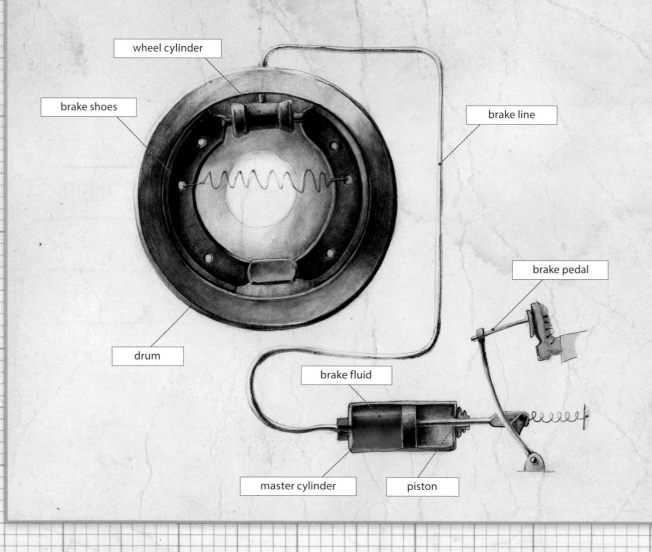

wheel cylinder

brake shoes

brake line

drum

brake pedal

brake fluid

master cylinder

piston

INSIDE THE BODY

Building the body of a car isn't easy. A wooden form needs to be built for each section of the bodywork. This wooden form is called a *buck*. After a buck has been made, a metal sheet is hammered around the wooden form. The buck gives each panel of metal its shape. Then, finally, these metal panels are welded together. Phew!

STEERING

For the driver the steering system is the most important part of the car. It's how the driver controls where the car will go. Every steering wheel is connected to a steering box. The steering box controls the gears that turn the wheels. The tie rod makes sure that when you steer right your cars' tires do too!

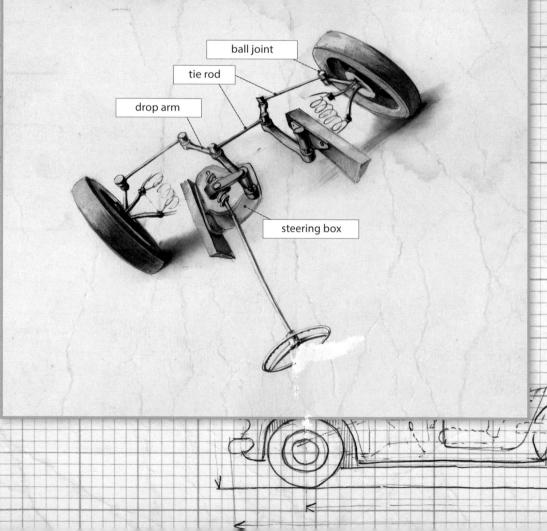

ball joint

tie rod

drop arm

steering box

STEERING BOX

rocker shaft

steering nut

worm gear

drop arm

HOW TO BUILD A CAR IN 5 STEPS

1

DREAM

Think hard. Do you really want to build a car? Even though it may take a long, long time? Then go for it, buddy!

2

BUILD THE FRAME

Make sure you have all the necessary parts and pieces before you start building. Otherwise, you might be stuck with a car that only has three wheels! And remember, the frame is the skeleton of the car. It needs to be built first.

BUILD THE ENGINE

This is where things get tricky. Learn as much as you can about how engines work. Pretty soon you'll be a regular ol' Phoebe.

3

BUILD THE BODY

You're almost done—well, sort of. Each piece of the body needs to be welded together. Make sure your measurements are precise! Otherwise, you could have a lopsided car on your hands.

4

HIT THE ROAD!

You've done it. Live large in the car that you made with your own bare hands. It's joyride o'clock!

5

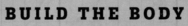

ELI'S NEW DREAM